Witness to History

The Great Depression

Nathaniel Harris

Heinemann Library
Chicago, Illinois

Designed by Heinemann Library
Produced for Heinemann by Discovery Books Ltd
Originated by Ambassador Litho Ltd
Printed and bound in China
by South China Printing

07 06 05 04 03
10 9 8 7 6 5 4 3 2 1

**Library of Congress Cataloging-in-Publication
Data**

Harris, Nathaniel.
   The Great Depression / Nathaniel Harris.
      p. cm. -- (Witness to history)
Summary: Describes the Great Depression or 1929-
1941 and its impact on
the United States and other areas of the world.
   ISBN 1-4034-4568-0 (HC) -- ISBN 1-4034-4576-1
(pbk.)
   1. Depressions--1929. 2. Depressions--1929--
Europe. 3.
Depressions--1929--United States. 4. Economic
history--1918-1945. [1.
Depressions--1929. 2. Depressions--1929--United
States. 3.
Depressions--1929--Europe. 4. Economic history--
1918-1945.] I. Title.
II. Witness to history (Heinemann Library (Firm)).
   HB37171929 .H34 2003
   330.9'043--dc21
                              2003007109

Acknowledgments
The author and publishers are grateful to the
following for permission to reproduce copyright
material:

pp. 4, 5, 14, 15, 25, 29, 35, 36, 38, 39, 44, 46 Peter
Newark's Pictures; p. 6 Christopher Felver/CORB
pp. 8, 9, 10, 23, 24, 28, 32, 34, 37 Bettmann/CORBIS
pp. 11, 27, 49 Hulton-Deutsch Collection/CORBIS
pp. 12, 16, 20, 22, 40, 42 Mary Evans Picture Libra
pp. 13, 18, 19 Getty Images; pp. 17, 26, 48 CORBIS;
30 Underwood & Underwood/CORBIS; p. 50 Eye
Ubiquitous/CORBIS.

Cover photograph of men eating soup during the
Great Depression in the United States reproduce
with permission of Bettmann/CORBIS.

The publishers would like to thank Bob Rees,
historian and teacher, for his assistance in the
preparation of this book.

Some words are shown in
bold, **like this.** You can find
out what they mean by lookir
in the glossary.

Contents

Introduction

The Great Depression was an economic collapse that affected most countries in the world between 1929 and 1941. Businesses went **bankrupt.** Factories and banks closed. Farmers received ruinously low prices for their produce. Fewer goods were manufactured and traded between nations. The most devastating impact of the Great Depression, however, was on the lives of ordinary people. Millions of people lost their jobs. Many were out of work for years. They were poor and often did not have enough to eat. Some became homeless and either lived in makeshift **shantytowns** or kept on the move, hoping to find jobs or shelter somewhere else.

The Great Depression started in the United States with the Wall Street Crash, a financial crisis (see page 14). Then, it spread rapidly throughout the global economy. People who lived through it were stunned, but they were also puzzled. How could so many people be jobless when machines lay idle and goods of all sorts were obviously needed? Of course, there had been good and bad times before—at their most extreme, **booms** (periods of great **prosperity**) and **slumps** (severe falls in production, trade, and employment). But the Depression was different. It affected the entire world and dragged on and on.

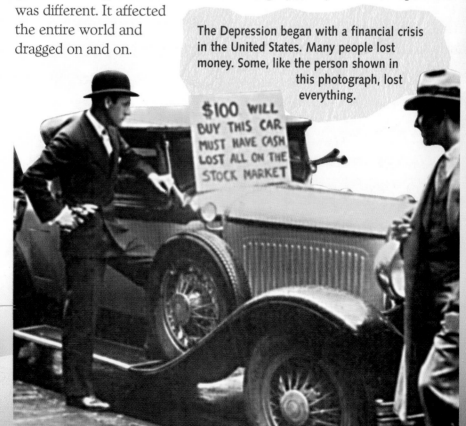

The Depression began with a financial crisis in the United States. Many people lost money. Some, like the person shown in this photograph, lost everything.

$100 WILL BUY THIS CAR MUST HAVE CASH LOST ALL ON THE STOCK MARKET

The Depression hit its peak in 1933. Here, hungry, unemployed men in Chicago line up for a free cup of coffee and a doughnut.

A troubled world

The world's major economic system—**capitalism**—appeared to have failed, and governments seemed to be powerless. Only a few leaders—notably President Franklin D. Roosevelt—took dramatic action that gave people hope again. By contrast, in Europe—which had often been troubled since the upheavals of World War I (1914–1918)—the Depression created discontent. In some places, it encouraged new and different economic forces. The government and economy of Soviet Russia (the Soviet Union or **U.S.S.R.**) was based on **communism,** an economic system that claimed to create a society run by and for working people (see page 40). Communists in other countries worked to overthrow their governments, hoping to set up states like the Soviet Union. Even more threatening were the **fascist** movements that rejected **democracy** and glorified strong leadership and warlike ideas, and which sprang up in the 1930s (see page 38). In Germany, the **Nazi Party**—led by Adolf Hitler—became increasingly popular as the Depression worsened. People were vulnerable and desperate, and Hitler's charisma and confidence no doubt appealed to many of them. When Hitler took power in 1933, Europe began a slide toward war that would eventually engulf the world and, at a terrible price, end the Depression.

How Do We Know?

Vast quantities of materials that relate to the Great Depression have survived. These materials include books, magazines, newspapers, advertisements, films, radio programs, written and taped interviews, works of art, and even manufactured objects. Such sources fall into two types. Secondary sources, including books, articles, and documentary films, describe and interpret the available evidence. They may be factually correct, but the facts have been chosen by the author and are likely to reflect his or her point of view or **prejudices.**

Oral historian Studs Terkel conducted hundreds of interviews with survivors of the Depression for his book **Hard Times.** He was careful to talk to men and women of different races and classes.

Primary sources contain direct evidence—for example, the actual words of Depression victims—written down or recorded by an interviewer. The Depression is rich in this type of oral, or spoken, history, since large numbers of people were interviewed at the time or in later years. Oral evidence gives us a clear idea of the social history of the Depression—how people lived through it, their hardships, and their varied stories. There are also many other primary sources about the history of the Depression, including **manuscripts** and documents, newspaper articles, autobiographies, photographs, newsreels, and sound recordings.

Weighing the evidence

Primary sources provide valuable direct evidence, but they have to be used with care. Even accounts given by eyewitnesses are not necessarily reliable. They may be deliberately misleading. Or they may be influenced by the eyewitnesses' prejudices. **Testimony** given years after an event is likely to be affected by fading memories and the impact of more recent experiences. Even objects can be misinterpreted; for example, the pictures in a millionaire's photo album might be filled with useful information, but they are not likely to give us an accurate idea of how most people lived at the time. Historians try to weigh the evidence, and they are likely to believe a source to be most convincing when it is backed up by similar evidence taken from a variety of other sources.

Primary sources are particularly good at telling us how large groups of people lived. Establishing the truth about political history can be trickier. Even where the basic facts are well documented, there are often widely different opinions about why decisions were made and what the political leaders were aiming to achieve. Matters of economics and finance are also hard to interpret. Even today, economists argue about why the Depression happened and why it went on for such a long time. **Statistics** rarely tell the full story and can be interpreted—or twisted—in various ways. For all of these reasons, history can never be an exact science. But it remains excitingly open to new ideas and interpretations.

The U.S. Boom

By the 1920s, the United States was the most economically powerful country in the world. It was a vast land with great industries and huge resources. The **prosperity** of the United States made a striking contrast with the economic situation of Europe, which had been hard hit during World War I (1914–1918). The United States had taken part in the war, but had entered late and suffered less. In fact, U.S. industries received a great boost from the demand for war materials.

In the 1920s, the United States became more prosperous than ever before largely thanks to mass-production techniques, such as those used to make Ford automobiles cheap enough for millions of people to buy. Buying was easier than ever, too, as rent-to-own and other credit programs flourished.

This prosperity was uneven, however, and more fragile than it seemed. There were still many poor people. Falling food prices hurt farmers during the 1920s. Many workers had gone into debt in order to buy goods, and many companies had borrowed heavily. None of this seemed too serious—until the cracks began to show in the financial world.

These wealthy U.S. citizens of the 1920s thought the good times would never end. This group is enjoying a wet lunch in the hotel atmosphere of the Huntington Pool in Los Angeles.

The 15 millionth Ford automobile rolled off the production line in 1927. The United States was the first country in which cars were owned by large numbers of ordinary people.

Herbert Hoover's speech

Below is the inaugural address, or speech given by a new president when sworn in, made by Herbert Hoover on March 4, 1929. He stresses the prosperity and security of life in the U.S.

If we survey the situation of our Nation both at home and abroad, we find many satisfactions. . . . We have emerged from the losses of the Great War [World War I] and the reconstruction following it . . . we have contributed to the recovery and progress of the world. What America has done has given renewed hope and courage to all who have faith in government by the people. In the large view, we have reached a higher degree of comfort and security than ever existed before in the history of the world. Through liberation from widespread poverty we have reached a higher degree of individual freedom than ever before. . . .

Ours is a land rich in resources; stimulating in its glorious beauty; filled with millions of happy homes; blessed with comfort and opportunity. In no nation are the institutions of progress more advanced. In no nation are the fruits of accomplishment more secure. In no nation is the government more worthy of respect. No country is more loved by its people. . . . I have no fears for the future of our country. It is bright with hope.

Wall Street

All big companies need large sums of money to run their operations. Most of them raise it by issuing and selling thousands of **shares,** or stock. Shares are certificates that make the holder a part-owner, or **investor,** in the company. **Shareholders** regularly receive part of the company's profits, called a **dividend.** They can also make money from their shares by selling them if they rise in value. The value of shares is affected by the expected size of dividends. But the value is also strongly affected by other factors, such as optimism or gloom about business in general. In the 1920s, American citizens were full of optimism and the price of shares rose again and again.

The New York **Stock Exchange** on Wall Street is the main place in the United States where shares are issued, bought, and sold; it is often called "Wall Street" for short. By 1929, people were buying shares on Wall Street in a frenzy that drove prices higher and higher. It seemed as if all a person had to do was buy shares, and riches would follow automatically.

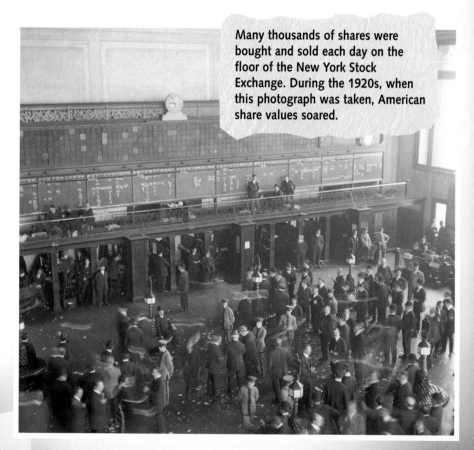

Many thousands of shares were bought and sold each day on the floor of the New York Stock Exchange. During the 1920s, when this photograph was taken, American share values soared.

John J. Raskob's interview

In August 1929, John J. Raskob, vice president of General Motors, was interviewed in the *Ladies' Home Journal.* The article, "Everybody Ought to Be Rich," appeared just three months before the Wall Street Crash and the start of the Depression.

Being rich is, of course, a comparative status. A man with a million dollars used to be considered rich, but so many people have at least that much these days, or are earning incomes in excess of a normal return from a million dollars, that a millionaire does not cause any comment. . . . In my opinion, the wealth of the country is bound to increase at a very rapid rate. . . . Anyone who believes that opportunities are now closed . . . is welcome to the opinion—and whatever increment [gain] it will bring. I think that we have scarcely started. . . . **Prosperity** is in the nature of an endless chain. . . .

If a man saves $15 a week and invests in good common stocks and allows the dividends and rights to accumulate, at the end of twenty years he will have at least $80,000 and an income from investments of around $400 a month. He will be rich.

John J. Raskob was a highly successful businessman who became vice president of General Motors.

And because income can do that, I am firm in my belief that anyone not only can be rich, but ought to be rich.

Post-War Europe

The Depression might have had less impact worldwide if the European economies had been stronger. They were very fragile, however, so any crisis in the U.S. was likely to produce a disastrous effect on them.

Before World War I, Europe had been prosperous and economically stable. The war exhausted the winners in Europe—Great Britain and France—and left them with heavy war debts. The losers—Germany and its allies—were even worse off. There were revolutionary upheavals in many countries. The German emperor fled, and a republic was set up. However, the Germans were still faced with paying huge **reparations**—compensation for the wartime damage inflicted by the German armies. The winners forced Germany to agree to these reparations when peace was made by the Treaty of Versailles in 1919. Then, in 1923, Germany endured a new crisis: soaring **inflation** made German currency almost worthless, wiping out many people's savings.

In the mid-1920s, the European economy seemed to be reviving. But loans from the U.S. were important, especially in Germany. If American **prosperity** faltered and the loans were withdrawn, Europe would be in trouble.

During the great German inflation of 1923, money had little value. Here, it is being weighed and traded as plain paper.

The French village of La Bassée was completely destroyed during World War I. Loss of life, destruction, and the huge cost of the war meant that economic recovery was slow and uncertain throughout Europe.

Dr. Frieda Wunderlich's account

Dr. Frieda Wunderlich, the editor of a scholarly journal, recalled the German inflation of 1923 when the value of money dropped in a matter of hours or even minutes.

As soon as I received my salary I rushed out to buy the daily necessities. My daily salary, as editor . . . was just enough to buy one loaf of bread and a small piece of cheese or some oatmeal. On one occasion I had to refuse to give a lecture at a Berlin city college because I could not be assured that my fee would cover the subway fare to the classroom, and it was too far to walk. On another occasion, a private lesson I gave to the wife of a farmer was paid somewhat better—by one loaf of bread for the hour.

An acquaintance of mine, a clergyman, came to Berlin from a suburb with his monthly salary to buy a pair of shoes for his baby; he could buy only a cup of coffee. The Zeiss Works in Jena, a **nonprofit** enterprise [business], calculated its average wage paid during a week in November 1923 and found weekly earnings to be worth four gold marks [units of German currency], less than a sixth of prewar levels.

The Crash

In the United States, the prices of **shares** soared for most of 1929. Yet, most shares were being bought and sold for far more than they were really worth. Sooner or later, their prices were bound to fall sharply. This fall might not have been disastrous if Wall Street had not had other weaknesses. But easy credit programs encouraged people to purchase more shares than they could afford, and groups of companies operated with very little **capital.** If the **boom** ended, the result could be very serious.

Early in September 1929, share prices peaked and then sagged. The situation became alarming on Black Thursday, October 24, when millions of shares changed hands and prices tumbled. The following week, panic set in. **Shareholders** tried desperately to sell, and prices collapsed. Many people lost all they had, whether fortunes or hard-earned life savings. The biggest drops were over by November, but prices drifted down for years, and by 1932 shares were worth only a fraction of their value before the Crash.

The Crash began October 24, 1929. Huge crowds gathered outside the New York Stock Exchange on Wall Street, fascinated or fearful as the news of plunging share prices spread.

1929

The bad news continued. The **New York Times** of October 30, 1929, told of another disastrous day (October 29) on Wall Street.

A report from the New York Times

On the day following Black Thursday, October 24, 1929, an article in the *New York Times* described the frenzy and panic that gripped Wall Street that day.

The most disastrous decline in the biggest and broadest stock market of history rocked the financial district yesterday. . . . It carried down with it **speculators,** big and little, in every part of the country, wiping out thousands of accounts. It is probable that if the stockholders of the country's foremost corporations had not been calmed by the attitude of leading bankers and the subsequent rally, the business of the country would have been seriously affected. . . . The total losses cannot be accurately calculated because of the large number of markets and the thousands of securities not listed. . . . However, they were staggering, running into billions of dollars. Fear struck the big speculators and little ones, big **investors** and little ones. Thousands of them threw their holdings into the whirling Stock Exchange pit for what they would bring. Losses were tremendous and thousands of prosperous . . . accounts, sound and healthy a week ago, were completely wrecked in the strange **debacle,** due to a combination of circumstances, but accelerated into a crash by fear. . . . Wild-eyed speculators crowded the . . . offices, awed by the disaster which had overtaken many of them. . . .

15

The Depression Begins in the United States

The Wall Street Crash ruined a number of companies and many individuals. Then, instead of ending there, the damage spread into the wider economy, shattering entire industries and putting millions of people out of work. This happened partly because the crash showed the weaknesses of the economy. It also destroyed people's confidence in investments and savings, and that made things far worse.

Banks and their customers were early victims. After the crash, fearful people rushed to take their money out of banks. Banks that could not pay everyone immediately were forced to close down. Most banks had lent out part of the money that savers had left with them. In 1930 alone, over a thousand banks failed in this way. Meanwhile, the banks tried to get money back by canceling the loans they had made to businesses and farmers. Both groups were already in trouble, and demands for repayment caused a wave of **bankruptcies.** Shops and factories shut down, and workers lost their jobs. A chain reaction began in which jobless workers bought fewer goods, and falling demand led to yet more closures. The Great Depression had begun in earnest.

Thousands of banks failed during the Depression. This photo, taken in December 1930, shows the Brooklyn branch of the Bank of the United States closing its doors. The bank was unable to pay everyone who wanted their money.

16

President Herbert Hoover speaks to a group of journalists. Hoover frequently predicted—wrongly—that the Depression was about to end.

Edmund Wilson's report
Edmund Wilson, a famous American writer, investigated and reported on many Depression stories, including this tragedy of ruin and desperation.

Peter Romano . . . got something the matter with his chest and wasn't able to work any more. He sold his business and put the money into Wall Street.

When the Wall Street Crash came, Peter Romano lost almost everything. And by the time that Mrs. Romano had had a baby . . . and had afterward come down with pneumonia, he found he had only a few dollars left.

By June, he owed his landlord two months' rent. . . . The landlord, Antonio Copace . . . was insistent about the rent. Peter Romano . . . went to Mr. Copace with $26—one month's rent. But the old man refused it with fury and said that unless he got the whole sum right away, he would have the Romanos ejected [thrown out]. On June 11, he came himself to the Romanos. . . . He threatened to put them out that very afternoon. . . . Mrs. Romano went out in a final desperate effort to get together $52.

When she came back empty-handed, she found a lot of people outside the house, and upstairs, the police in her flat [apartment]. Peter had shot Mr. Copace and killed him, and was just being taken off to jail.

World in Crisis

The Wall Street Crash had an immediate impact almost everywhere. **Share** prices fell sharply on **stock exchanges** in Europe. People in the United States who were in financial difficulties withdrew the loans they had made to European countries. The result—falling output and lost jobs—was particularly severe in Germany. The situation was at least as bad for countries whose economies were based on **primary production**—non-manufactured goods such as foodstuffs and raw materials. Fear that the United States would not be able to afford their products led to much lower prices for East European grain, Brazilian coffee, Chilean copper, and many other goods.

Standards of living in these primary-producing countries fell, and they bought fewer manufactured goods. Industrialized countries were

able to **export** less, and trade between nations shrank. Countries tried to protect home industries and businesses. To ensure that they could at least sell to their own people, governments put taxes, known as **tariffs,** on **imports.** The result, all through the 1930s, was a shrinking of world trade that prolonged the Depression.

An unemployed man in Wigan, England, slumps against a corner while children stare curiously at him.

Fernando Liborio's description

Fernando Liborio, interviewed for the television series *People's Century,* described what it was like to be a 13-year-old Chilean worker and how the Depression affected Chile's copper-mining industry.

I started working in the year 1929. I was a 13-year-old child. I got a permit that increased my age by five years so that I could work. I worked as a weigher in a copper mine. . . . Times were wonderful. . . . There was work everywhere.

When the crash happened in the United States, quite honestly nothing like it had ever been known before. It was as if you were walking down the street and suddenly something hit you. To us, it all seemed very remote, miles away. New York was a long way off. But when your own boss tells you you haven't got a job anymore, then you really felt it . . . the owner of the mine called us and he said, "Children, the mine is going to stop because nobody is going to buy copper." But he said he would maintain the job places for one year . . . he knew we had not saved any money. We had spent all our money because we thought this would never occur. And when it happened it caught us without any savings. So, he kept us for one year, even if he didn't have anybody to buy the copper. He was an excellent **patrón.**

In 1930, this British man walked the streets with his sign. Millions of people had similar stories to tell.

I KNOW 3 TRADES
I SPEAK 3 LANGUAGES
FOUGHT FOR 3 YEARS
HAVE 3 CHILDREN
AND NO WORK FOR
3 MONTHS
BUT I ONLY WANT
ONE JOB

19

Great Britain in the 1920s

World War I ended in 1918, and Great Britain was one of the victors. The cost of the war had greatly weakened the economy, however. Many resources—for example, **shares** in foreign industries—had been sold off, and Britain was deep in debt to the United States. Although still a leading industrial power, Britain was having trouble because long-established industries—such as textiles—were becoming run-down and out of date.

Even at the height of British **prosperity,** there had been slum-filled areas where poverty never went away. Despite government promises of "homes fit for heroes," little was done, and many who had fought in World War I felt betrayed. The British economy was shaky throughout the 1920s, and bitter struggles took place between workers and employers. These ended in 1926, when a **general strike** was defeated and workers were forced to accept wage cuts. Others were even worse off, and had no jobs at all. In the post-war years—before the Depression—there were never less than one million people without work. Like Germany, Britain was ill-equipped to face a world economic downturn.

When transportation workers took part in the general strike, police protection was needed for the volunteers who kept buses and trains running.

Wal Hannington's account

This passage from Wal Hannington's book *Never on Our Knees* shows that unemployment was an issue in Great Britain as early as 1922. It describes a demonstration held in London on Remembrance Day (November 11, commemorating the dead of World War I).

The London District Council of the N.U.W.M. [National Unemployed Workers' Movement] decided to organize a procession of unemployed—mainly ex-servicemen—to march to Whitehall [site of British government buildings] to honor their fallen comrades and to bring before the thousands of onlookers the plight [concerns] of the survivors. . . . I was in London for this event.

Our men started marching with bands and banners early in the morning from all the London boroughs to join up before 11 A.M. on the Thames Embankment. Toward the end of the official ceremony they formed one huge procession over 20,000 strong. . . . On the breasts of our men were displayed their own medals, but pinned to the banners of the local sections were hundreds of medals of their comrades who had died since the war or who were too crippled or ill to join in the march.

Then, just before we entered Whitehall, hundreds of our men took **pawn** tickets from their pockets and pinned them on their coats for the densely packed crowds to witness . . . when the covering was removed from the large wreath being carried at the head of our procession the inscription stood out bold and clear: "From the living victims, the unemployed, to our dead comrades who died in vain [without purpose]."

Helping Handouts

People without jobs were liable to lose their homes, and might even starve. One source of support was the family, if any of its members were working. Also important for huge numbers of the unemployed was help from the community. Some countries in western Europe, such as Great Britain and Germany, had state-run **social security** programs. These programs offered weekly welfare payments (also known as relief or the dole) to workers when they were sick or unemployed. During the Depression, the dole, though small, kept most families from complete despair. People became deeply resentful when cost-cutting governments attempted to reduce the dole (see page 30).

These British women are in line to claim welfare payments provided by the state and local authorities.

In 1929, the federal government of the United States had not yet established social security programs. The unemployed were dependent on local programs, where they existed, and the heroic efforts of private charities. Huge lines formed at soup kitchens, where hot soup and bread or coffee and doughnuts were handed out. President Herbert Hoover (1929–1933) became unpopular because people felt—perhaps unfairly—that he was doing too little to help. It was not until President Roosevelt introduced the New Deal (see page 36), which involved federal authorities for the first time, that large-scale relief was provided.

Max Cohen's experiences

In his book *I Was One of the Unemployed*, the British writer Max Cohen recalled his experiences as a 20-year-old trying to survive on the dole.

You leave the Labor Exchange [social security office] on Friday and you have in your pocket a ten-shilling note [75¢] and half a crown [40¢] . . . you must make do until one more week has passed. . . .

Little things, that a person who is earning wages scarcely bothers about, have now assumed great moment [importance]. . . . Maybe your shoe-laces have broken and been tied together and broken again . . . . Maybe your razor blade will no longer shave you. . . . Possibly you need a haircut. . . . Your trousers are falling to pieces. . . . It is raining. . . . Your shoes are cracked beyond repair. . . . These are mere trifles.

The question, the main question, is what food you should buy, and how much—or little—of it. . . .

Maybe you have been going hungry for the last few days. . . . Strange temptations and desires assail you. . . .

There is more even than this. You want to go somewhere bright and gay, lively and happy. . . . You would like—whisper it—to go to the pictures [movies] this afternoon.

But there is stern reality and you must face it. . . . Better go home. At the grocery shop choose . . . the cheapest foods on which you can make some pretense of living.

Breadlines and soup kitchens offered some nourishment to the poor and unemployed in the United States.

On the Move

During the Depression many people lost their homes or were forced to leave them and look for work elsewhere. Many unemployed families could not afford to make the payments on their houses or farms and were **evicted.** The lucky ones found cheaper places, but thousands went to live in **shantytowns** or took to the road.

Shantytowns consisted of shacks built from materials such as cardboard. They were found all over the world, often on the edge of large cities. In the United States they were known as Hoovervilles, a mocking reference to the unpopular president Herbert Hoover. In large countries such as the United States and Australia, there were also many people on the move, hoping to find a better life in a new place. In the United States, their numbers grew because drought had turned parts of the Great Plains—a large farming area in the middle of the country—into a dry, exhausted Dust Bowl. This, and the increasing use of machines instead of human labor in agriculture, set thousands of people moving west toward California.

This shantytown of shacks was built by the homeless in Seattle. These Hoovervilles sprang up in many parts of the country.

Paul Taylor's article

The plight of migrants from the Great Plains attracted international attention. The article "Again the Covered Wagon," by Paul Taylor, appeared in the July 1935 issue of *Survey Graphic* magazine.

A farmer has loaded his possessions onto his automobile as he prepares to leave the Dust Bowl in search of a better life.

Vast clouds of dust rise and roll across the Great Plains. . . . Exposed by cultivation which killed the protecting grasses, and powdered by protracted [long] drought, the rich topsoil is being stripped from tens of thousands of acres by wind erosion, leaving land and life impoverished. Dust, drought, and protracted depression have exposed also the human resources of the plains. . . . After the drifting dust clouds drift the people. . . .

The refugees travel in old automobiles and light trucks, some of them home-made, and frequently with trailers behind. All their worldly possessions are piled on the car and covered with old canvas or ragged bedding, with perhaps bedsprings atop, a small iron cook-stove on the running board, a battered trunk, lantern, and galvanized iron washtub tied on behind. Children, aunts, grandmothers, and a dog are jammed into the car, stretching its capacity incredibly. . . .

It is hope that draws the refugees to California. . . . "All I want is a chance to make an honest living." . . .

Many families comfort themselves with the thought of returning home when drought and depression are over. Many will return, but many others will not; they have burned their bridges without realizing it. Now the movement is west. . . . "What bothers us travelin' people most is we can't get no place to stay still."

The Lives of Women

In most countries, the traditional role of women was very limited. They could take humble jobs as servants or laundresses, but most looked after the home and children while the men did the paid work. By 1900, however, women in the United States, Great Britain, and a few other countries were moving into other occupations, especially office work. During World War I, when millions of men were called into the armed forces, women took their places and showed that they could master all kinds of jobs.

In the 1920s, some women managed to keep their new independence, although they seldom earned as much as men doing the same kind of work. During the Depression, women were sometimes employed just because they could be paid less then men. Successful and famous women, like President Roosevelt's politically active wife Eleanor or the British pilot Amy Johnson, were exceptions. And in some places, notably **Nazi** Germany (see page 38), there was renewed emphasis on the idea that a woman's place was in the home. In the wealthier countries, conveniences such as vacuum cleaners and radios did make the home a more pleasant place. But, for women everywhere, the Depression made familiar problems of housekeeping and feeding and clothing their families even more difficult.

Recorded by Dorothea Lange, a famous documentary photographer whose pictures helped people understand the victims of the Depression, this careworn mother of three children was part of a farm family on the move in the United States.

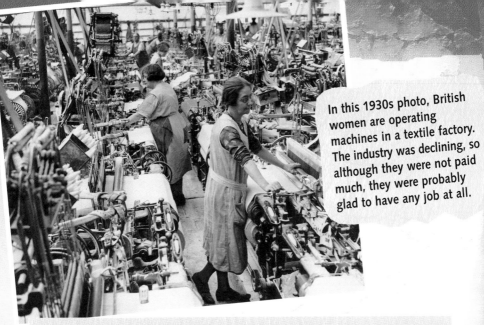

In this 1930s photo, British women are operating machines in a textile factory. The industry was declining, so although they were not paid much, they were probably glad to have any job at all.

A housewife's interview

This Scottish housewife was one of many subjects interviewed in Margery Spring Rice's *Working-Class Women*, published in 1939.

Mrs. MacN. of Glasgow, lives in one room and kitchen. She says it has no drawbacks. "I take everything as it comes, and the only difficulty is when baby is restless." Her husband is an unemployed carter, and she gets £2 [$3.00] unemployment money and 10 shillings [75¢] from one boy (aged 16) who is working. Out of this . . . she pays 9 shillings [67¢] rent. She is 37 and has had 14 pregnancies, which include four children who have died and two miscarriages; there are therefore eight living children; five boys and two girls living at home. . . . She is "never ill unless with children, and that passed off comfortably." She gets up at 6 and goes to bed at 10. Her leisure consists of "15 minutes around the block with baby till he goes to sleep; 15 minutes for messages [shopping] at 2 P.M., Club gymnasium on Tuesday, 45 minutes, and sewing class Thursday one hour or so." Porridge and milk and vegetable soups are regular items of diet. The visitor who saw her says, "This woman . . . plans her time very methodically and manages to feed herself and her family sufficiently well to maintain health." The Scots are truly a wonderful people.

Continuing Collapse

For a time after the Wall Street Crash, countries struggled to weather the storm. However, 1931 was a terrible year. In June, a large Austrian bank, the Kredit Anstalt, failed. The threat of a Central European collapse prompted the United States to suspend the collection of war debts (money owed from World War I), but it was too late. In Germany, already in a situation of emergency, a wave of bank failures led to a breakup of the economy. By late 1932, the number of unemployed Germans reached a staggering 8 million. Soon afterward, Great Britain was hit by a financial crisis, and France, little affected until then, began to suffer from the Depression. Unemployment in the United States soared, reaching about 12 million—and still rising—by the end of 1932.

One way in which people expressed their discontent was through voting. In Germany, the communist and **Nazi** parties gained support. The Nazis eventually took power (see page 38). In the United States, President Hoover became increasingly unpopular. In the presidential elections of November 1932, an overwhelming majority of people voted for Franklin Delano Roosevelt, who promised them what he called a "New Deal."

Franklin Delano Roosevelt, campaigning for the presidency in 1932, shakes hands with a miner. Roosevelt presented himself as the champion of ordinary working people, and most of them voted for the New Deal he promised.

Christopher Isherwood's account

The British writer Christopher Isherwood witnessed the events in Germany and recorded them in his novel *Goodbye to Berlin*. Here, he describes the impact of the bank collapse.

Next morning, Frl. [Miss] Schroeder [his landlady] woke me in great excitement:

"Herr [Mr.] Issyvoo [Isherwood], what do you think? They've shut the Darmstadter und National! There'll be thousands ruined, I shouldn't wonder! The milkman says we'll have civil war in a fortnight! Whatever do you say to that!"

As soon as I'd got dressed, I went down into the street. Sure enough, there was a crowd outside the branch bank on the Nollendorfplatz corner, a lot of men with leather satchels and women with string-bags—women like Frl. Schroeder herself. The iron lattices were drawn down over the bank windows.

"Work" (arbeit) and "bread" (brot) are the key words in this Nazi propaganda poster. The Nazis' success in creating jobs made them popular and blinded people to their oppressive policies.

Most of the people were staring intently and rather stupidly at the locked door. In the middle of the door was fixed a small notice, beautifully printed. . . . The notice said that the Reichspresident [German president] had guaranteed the deposits. Everything was quite all right. Only the bank wasn't going to open. . . .

The details of the new emergency decrees were in the early evening papers—terse [short], governmentally inspired. One alarmist headline stood out boldly, barred with blood-red ink: "Everything collapses!"

29

Tackling the Crisis

Ever since the Great Depression, governments have been blamed for doing too little about the crisis. But they had only followed the accepted economic theories of the time, which insisted that a government should not spend more than its income. This is known as a balanced budget. The theories said that if the Depression reduced the government's income, it should cut spending, for example, by lowering welfare benefits and the wages of state employees.

The chief critic of these ideas was a British economist, John Maynard Keynes, who argued that a balanced budget was not a top priority in a Depression. In fact, he said, governments should borrow money and spend large sums on public projects: building roads, for example. These projects would give workers jobs and wages to spend. The workers' ability to buy would stimulate industry to increase production—which would create even more jobs. The economic machine would get into gear again, reversing the effects of the Depression.

Keynes's ideas were not generally accepted at the time, although some governments experimented with increased spending at the height of the Depression, and his ideas probably had some influence on the New Deal (see page 36).

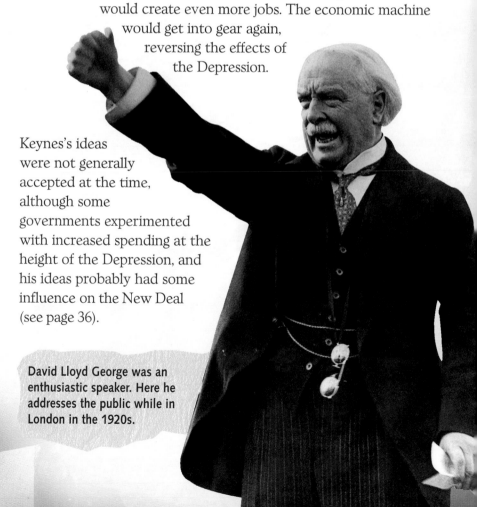

David Lloyd George was an enthusiastic speaker. Here he addresses the public while in London in the 1920s.

David Lloyd George's extract

Former British Prime Minister David Lloyd George proposed a program of public works to remedy unemployment in 1929, before the Depression struck. His Liberal Party failed to win the election that year, however, and its policies were never tested.

The nation has lost confidence in the present Government. Its complete failure to grapple with the serious emergency in our trade and the consequent abnormal unemployment has created a general sense of disappointment in all classes of the community. . . . The central domestic issue which confronts us is unemployment. There can be no national health, no widespread prosperity, there can be no national happiness and contentment so long as more than a million of our fellow-countrymen are unable to find work and earn wages by their work. . . .

It [the Liberal Party] pledges itself to find immediate employment for those now out of work on works of national utility and development, many of these works, like electricity, telephones, housing, roads, and railways, being long overdue. It is surely better, instead of wasting our substance by spending £70,000,000 [$100 million] a year on "doles" for which there is no return, to lay out this enormous expenditure in providing work on plans which will leave the nation richer and more efficient for its tasks.

Great Britain during the Depression

In 1929, a Labor Party government took office, pledging to combat the existing unemployment problem. Little was achieved, however, before Britain, like other countries, began to feel the effects of the Wall Street Crash. Britain's **exports** of manufactured goods were vital to its **prosperity.** Countries producing food and raw materials were hard hit by the Depression, however, and could no longer afford to buy as many British goods. Unemployment in Britain, already high, soared. It eventually peaked at almost three million, nearly a quarter of all registered workers.

The Labor government followed accepted economic theory and refused to spend public money in order to create jobs. By 1931, a special committee was recommending that government spending should actually be cut. After a political crisis, the cuts were carried out in September 1931 by a new government. Employees of the state, such as civil servants, teachers, soldiers, and sailors, had to take lower wages. An unpopular means test (an investigation of family income) kept payments to the unemployed low. The Depression—also known as the **Slump** in Britain—took hold, bringing misery to millions of people.

G. Rees's memories

These memories of a Welsh man, G. Rees, were recorded by the British Broadcasting Corporation (BBC). Contrast his account of a town where over 60 percent of the workforce was unemployed with J.B. Priestley's account on page 43.

I remember walking through the streets . . . near Merthyr [Merthyr Tydfil, an industrial town in Wales]—and being amazed simply by the number of people there were in it. The street was simply crowded and you could hardly move. The extraordinary thing about it was that the people were not doing anything—they were not moving, they were leaning against lamp posts, smoking cigarettes—those who had some—almost immobile, as if they were turned to stone, and I suddenly realized that this was what went on every day of the week in Merthyr. The entire population was unemployed and that is almost literally true, apart from the shopkeepers, and they were giving credit to people who couldn't afford it, and this was really like seeing a world turned into stone, absolutely dead. And as far as one could see, without any hope whatever of ever reviving again.

King Edward VIII visited Pontypool, Wales, in November 1936. The living conditions of the unemployed shocked him, but promises of action came to nothing when he gave up his right to the throne soon afterward.

Protest

Millions of people were impoverished by the Depression. Many were angry, believing their governments could have done more to help. Some of the unemployed and hungry felt defeated and lacked the energy to act. Others joined political movements. More protested in other ways.

Protest took a variety of forms. People often organized marches to publicize their problems. One of the biggest of these marches was the Bonus Army march in 1932. Twenty thousand American veterans of World War I converged on Washington, D.C., demanding the bonuses they had been promised by the government for their wartime service. They camped outside the city until their **shantytown** was destroyed by American troops and they were driven away. At Invergordon in Great Britain, sailors went on **strike** in 1931 to fight savage pay cuts. They won some concessions, or agreements to help, from the government.

In Britain there were a number of hunger marches on London. The most famous was made in 1936 from the town of Jarrow in an attempt to demand government help. Little was done for Jarrow. Marches stirred up sympathy, but governments generally refused to change their policies.

The shacks of the Bonus Army were burned on July 28, 1932. World War I veterans marched on Washington, D.C., demanding their promised bonuses for wartime service. American troops scattered them and burned down their camp.

The Jarrow marchers were unemployed men from Jarrow in northeastern England. In 1936, they tramped to London to publicize the town's troubles. The woman is one of the organizers, Ellen Wilkinson, a political representative of Jarrow.

Ellen Wilkinson's experience

Ellen Wilkinson, a political representative of Jarrow in northeastern England, was one of the organizers of the Jarrow march. In her book, *The Town that was Murdered*, she described the warm welcome the marchers received on their way.

A *few high spots stand out . . . wealthy Harrogate where the Territorial [Army] officers looked after us . . . Leeds where the chief newspaper proprietor gave us a meal the men still talk of . . . and with free beer! Barnsley, where Joseph Jones the miners' leader and Mayor—how we blessed him!—had the municipal baths all heated ready for the men, and where I had the muscle-easing luxury of the women's municipal foam bath. Or the awful days like the twenty-mile stretch from Bedford to Luton when it rained solidly all day, and the wind drove the rain in our teeth. Except for the hospitality at the end of the day, one day's tramp was much like another. The one thing that mattered was the weather. The men were up at 6:30, the cooks having got up earlier to prepare breakfast. They had all slept together on the bare boards of a school or drill hall . . . if lucky on palliasses [mattresses] borrowed from somewhere.*

The New Deal

On March 4, 1933, Franklin D. Roosevelt became president of the United States. He had promised the people a New Deal, and the first 100 days of his administration were action-packed. Among other things, American banks were rescued from a fresh panic. The New Deal mainly operated through government agencies set up to create jobs and help people. The Civilian Conservation Corps (CCC) hired hundreds of thousands of young men to plant trees and irrigate farmlands. The Tennessee Valley Authority (TVA) built dams that were great feats of engineering, and which transformed the region. And the Works Progress Administration (WPA) employed huge numbers of people to construct public buildings, bridges, highways, and parks. These public works had an immense impact on the face of the United States. They also made unemployed people feel better by giving them useful jobs as well as wages. Meanwhile, the state authorities were given help to provide relief for the poor. And, in 1935, the **Social Security** Act provided welfare benefits for the unemployed and the elderly.

Robert L. Miller's essay
Robert L. Miller enrolled in the Civilian Conservation Corps (CCC) when he was 22. He felt the experience made a man of him, and he wrote an enthusiastic essay, "It's a Great Life," in praise of it.

Roosevelt's measures were experimental, and not all of them worked. But, the numbers of unemployed did start to drop, and vigorous government action did much to revive the nation's optimism.

President Franklin D. Roosevelt is shown as he prepares to speak on the radio. His fireside chats became famous, making people feel they knew the president personally.

Roosevelt's Works Progress Administration (WPA) employed millions of out-of-work Americans on public projects. Here, a road is being widened by WPA employees.

When I finally enrolled . . . at Sacramento, California, in October, 1933, I was conscious of just one thing—I would be fed, clothed, and sheltered during the coming winter. Also, I would receive enough actual cash each month to provide the few luxuries I desired. . . .

I joined seventy other young men on the morning of October 26 to leave for our camp in the Sierra Nevada Mountains. Our arrival at camp that same evening was an event that I shall never forget. I was pleasantly surprised at the . . . genuine hospitality and good cheer that . . . reached out to greet we newcomers.

. . . by enrolling in president Roosevelt's peacetime army, I managed to retain my self-respect. I did not have to become either a parasite, living off my relatives, or a professional bum. In other words, it gave me a chance to stand on my own two feet and make my own way in the world.

Then it gave me the opportunity to make friendships that will live forever. . . . They are fine young men, those chaps who go into the forests of our country to do their bit to preserve our woods. . . .

The Dictators

In many parts of the world, the discontent bred by the Depression helped breed new political movements, now generally described as **fascist.** The leaders of these movements told people to blame their troubles on scapegoats—**communists** or minorities, such as Jews, or more democratic politicians. Strong leaders and military-style, single-party rule would, they claimed, make everything better. Fascist parties won limited support in most places. In Germany, however, fascism was spectacularly successful. There, the **Nazi Party,** led by Adolf Hitler, came to power in 1933. Trampling all opposition, Hitler re-armed Germany after World War I and began a policy of ruthless military expansion.

Nazi dictator Adolf Hitler responds to an adoring crowd. Such scenes were typical of fascist states, where propaganda presented leaders as godlike figures.

For fascist states, new military action had the advantage of taking attention away from problems at home, giving people a supposed enemy to hate and blame. Distracting the masses from the effects of the Depression was an important motive for fascist Italy's conquest of the African kingdom of Abyssinia (Ethiopia) in 1935, and for Japanese attacks on China starting in 1931. So, the aggressions of Germany, Italy, and Japan, which led to World War II, were closely linked with the Depression.

Albert Speer's account

Albert Speer, who became Hitler's architect and armaments minister, described how he, and later his mother, came to join the Nazis, misled by promises and carried away by the atmosphere of mass meetings.

Here, it seemed to me, was hope. Here were new ideals, a new understanding, new tasks. . . . The peril [danger] of communism . . . could be checked, Hitler persuaded us, and instead of hopeless unemployment, Germany could move toward economic recovery . . . Both Goebbels [a leading Nazi] and Hitler had understood how to unleash mass instincts at their meetings . . . they succeeded in [creating] a . . . mob whose opinions they could mold as they pleased. . . . To compensate for misery, insecurity, and hopelessness, this [mob] wallowed for hours at a time in obsessions, savagery, license . . . for a few short hours the personal unhappiness caused by the breakdown of the economy was replaced by a frenzy that demanded victims. And Hitler and Goebbels threw them the victims. By lashing out at their opponents and vilifying [slandering] the Jews they gave expression and direction to fierce, primal passions. . . .

It must have been during these months that my mother saw an SA [Nazi storm trooper] parade in the streets of Heidelberg. The sight of discipline in a time of chaos, the impression of energy in an atmosphere of universal hopelessness, seems to have won her over, also. At any rate, without ever having heard a speech or read a pamphlet, she joined the party.

In a victory for fascist aggression, local chiefs surrender to the Italian invaders of Abyssinia in 1935. Fascist states glorified war and conquest.

The Soviet Alternative

The dominant world economic system was known as **capitalism:** **capital** was mainly held and used by private individuals and firms. During the Depression, capitalism seemed to be breaking down. One different system was **communism,** based on the control and planned use of resources by the government. The only communist country at that time was the **U.S.S.R.** Apparently untouched by the Depression, its people were working hard to create new industries. The government's Five-Year Plan to develop the economy was claimed to be a huge success. Not surprisingly, many outside observers thought that in time, communism might replace capitalism.

It was true that the U.S.S.R. was making economic progress, although its plans were not always as successful as its leaders claimed. It was a relatively undeveloped country, and the Soviet leadership was driving the people hard to industrialize in record time—at a very high cost. **Standards of living** were kept low so all resources could be used to create factories and machinery. And what many observers failed to see, or made excuses for, was the harsh nature of the ruling party under its ruthless leader, Stalin.

Here, the second Five-Year Plan is announced in the U.S.S.R. in 1932. The first Five-Year Plan had created new industries and was claimed as a triumph for the U.S.S.R.'s communist system.

Joseph Stalin's speech

This is an extract from a speech made by the Soviet leader, Joseph Stalin, in January 1933. He described the achievements of the Soviet Union's first Five-Year Plan for the economy.

The fundamental [basic] task of the Five-Year Plan was to transfer our country, with its backward technology, onto the lines of modern technology.

The fundamental task was to convert the U.S.S.R. from an agrarian [agriculture-based] and weak country . . . into an industrial and powerful country. . . .

The [Communist] Party's confidence in the feasibility [possibility] of the Five-Year Plan and its faith in the working class was so strong that the party undertook the fulfillment of this task not in five years, but in four years.

What are the results of the Five-Year Plan in four years. . . ?

We did not have an iron and steel industry, the basis for the industrialization of the country. Now we have one.

We did not have a tractor industry. Now we have one.

We did not have a machine-tool industry. Now we have one.

We did not have a big modern chemical industry. Now we have one.

We did not have a real and big industry for the production of modern agricultural machinery. Now we have one.

We did not have an aircraft industry. Now we have one.

Great Britain's Writers

The Great Depression stirred the conscience of many British writers. They hoped that by describing the suffering the Depression caused they could inspire people and governments to do more to help. Some wrote novels and stories set during the Depression. For example, British author Walter Greenwood's novel *Love on the Dole* (1933) was closely based on his own experiences, describing the struggles of a young man as he tried to find work while falling in love and getting married.

Other British writers felt that the situation was too urgent for story-telling. A number of authors produced direct reports of what they had seen and experienced. The famous novelist and playwright J.B. Priestley published *English Journey* in 1934, which described what he had seen on his travels around the country. The poet Edwin Muir did the same for his land in *Scottish Journey* (1935). Another famous writer, George Orwell, left vivid accounts of his life among the very poor in *Down and Out in Paris and London* (1934) and *The Road to Wigan Pier* (1937).

This photograph of the English writer J.B. Priestley was taken around 1930. His book **English Journey** describes the conditions he found during his travels around the country.

An extract from *English Journey*
In the 19th and early 20th centuries, Britain had grown rich on smoke-spewing industries. In *English Journey*, J.B. Priestley found that the Depression could bring cleanliness—and that appearances could be deceptive.

When I was traveling in the Midlands on this journey, I met a woman I know who had just come back from this Blackburn district, which was her original home. She had not been back for some years. "It's awful," she said. "They've got no work at all. And I hardly recognized the place. It's all becoming *clean*. The smuts [sooty deposits] are wearing off because so few of the mills are working. The brick and stone are beginning to show through. I hardly knew the place." . . . She was genuinely distressed. . . . I am not sure that a stranger would guess that there was something desperately wrong with these towns. He would notice, of course, that many of the mill chimneys were innocent of [without] smoke. If he were an astute observer, he might notice the absence of heavy commercial traffic. . . . But that, I think, is about all. These Lancashire towns . . . have not the derelict [abandoned] look of some places elsewhere. . . . The streets are not filled with men dismally loafing about. . . . Everything that was there before the **slump,** except the businesses themselves, is struggling on . . . the whole town is there, just as it was, but not in the condition it was. Its life is suffering from a deep internal injury.

American Arts of the New-Deal Era

Many American writers, musicians, and artists became unemployed during the Great Depression, and one of the achievements of the New Deal was to harness their talents. The Federal Arts Project paid thousands of painters and sculptors to decorate public buildings. Many of their **frescoes** and other works can still be seen today. Composers and performers were taken on by the Federal Music Project; actors, directors, and stage personnel by the Federal Theater Project.

One aim of the projects was to make a wide-ranging record of life and traditions in the United States. Workers on the Federal Music Project recorded folk songs that might otherwise have been forgotten. The photographers of the Federal Arts Project captured places and people on film. And the Federal Writers' Project produced hundreds of books, including volumes that described every state and territory in the country.

Not all of the work was government sponsored. The famous *Let Us Now Praise Famous Men* was commissioned by a magazine. Movies also dealt with aspects of the Depression, as did novels such as John Steinbeck's *The Grapes of Wrath*.

This farmworker and his family, photographed by photographer Dorothea Lange in 1938, have taken to the road in search of work. Lange's Depression-era photographs became extremely well known.

James Agee's description
In *Let Us Now Praise Famous Men*, James Agee described the lives of poor Alabama farmers. This passage is about George Gudger, his wife, and his four small children.

Gudger . . . now [in 1936] works for Chester Boles, who lives two miles south of Cookstown. . . .

Gudger has no home, no land, no mule; none of the more important farming implements. He must get all these of his landlord [Boles]. Boles, for his share of the corn and cotton [produced by Gudger], also advances him rations money during four months of the year, March through June, and his fertilizer.

Gudger pays him back with his labor and with the labor of his family.

At the end of the season he pays him back further: with half his corn; with half his cotton; with half his cottonseed. Out of his own half of these crops he also pays him back the rations money, plus interest, and his share of the fertilizer, plus interest, and such other debts, plus interest, as he may have incurred.

What is left, once doctors' bills and other debts have been deducted, is his year's earnings. Gudger is a . . . half-cropper or **sharecropper.**

The Recovery Stalls

By 1935, there were signs of improvement. In the United States, unemployment began to fall in response to New Deal programs and the development of new industries. In Britain, new manufactures, notably automobiles and electrical goods, prospered. Unemployment remained high, but overall production increased, and, for those with work, life was better. German unemployment was also cut, through work-creating **Nazi** policies of rearmament and highway-building.

However, the recovery was far from complete. In 1937, President Roosevelt, thinking the worst was over, cut spending to get back to a balanced budget, which he still believed was necessary. His decision created a new crisis—the Roosevelt Depression—in which production fell and unemployment again reached 10 million. In Great Britain, the new industries were mainly located in the south of England. Large regions in the north and in Scotland, which were now known as Depressed or Special Areas, remained black spots where nearly the entire populations of some towns were unemployed. There was also a downturn in the German economy, which led the Nazis to try to solve their economic problems through war and conquest.

Adolf Hitler, the leader of Nazi Germany, moves a shovelful of dirt to start the construction of a highway in Frankfurt in 1933. Although the Nazi regime was brutal in many ways, their policies did create jobs.

Ben Isaacs' story

Prosperity ended for American businessman Ben Isaacs in the late 1920s. His fortunes did not fully recover until 1944. He told his story to the oral historian Studs Terkel.

Whenever I went to get a job, I couldn't get no job. I went around selling razor blades and shoelaces. There was a day I would go over all the streets and come home with fifty cents, making a sale. That kept going until 1940 . . . [then] the war started. Things start to get a little better. My wife found a job in a restaurant for $20 a week. Right away, I sent a letter to the relief people: I don't think I would need their help any more. I was disgusted with relief, so ashamed. I couldn't face it any more.

My next door neighbor found me a job in the factory where he was working. That time I was around 50. The man said, "We can't use you." They wouldn't hire nobody over 45. Two weeks later, this same man said, "Go tell Bill [the name of the foreman] I sent you. He'll hire you." They hire me. They gave me 60 cents an hour.

Another War

Throughout the 1930s, the Depression refused to go away. Levels of unemployment remained high, and production and international trade failed to make a complete recovery. Then, in September 1939, war broke out in Europe. **Nazi** Germany attacked Poland, and Great Britain and France declared war on Germany. Italy and the **U.S.S.R.** were drawn in, and when Japan attacked the United States in December 1941, the conflict became a world war.

This photo shows Pearl Harbor after the surprise Japanese air attack on December 6, 1941. The attack brought the U.S. into World War II. As in Britain, war completed the recovery from the Depression.

The war finally ended the Depression. Huge numbers of men enrolled in the armed forces. Industries expanded to meet the needs of war production, and more food was needed to ensure that people could survive even if they were cut off by enemy action. There was now a shortage of labor, and large numbers of women who had never before worked outside the home joined the workforce. In 1944, with victory approaching for the **alliance** of the U.S., U.S.S.R., and Britain, plans were made for a new economic order in which, it was hoped, the mistakes of the past would be avoided.

When World War II broke out in September 1939, everyone could find a job either in the armed forces or the factories. This photograph, taken in 1940, shows four-inch (10 cm) naval guns being manufactured.

Louis Banks' account

Louis Banks, an African American, left home at the age of 14. Unable to find a job, he had a difficult life for a long time. Here, we hear how he found security—in the middle of a war.

When the war came, I was so glad when I got in the army. I knew I was safe. I put a uniform on, and I said, "Now I'm safe." I had money comin', I had food comin', and I had a lot of a gang around me. I knew [if I were] on the streets or hoboing [being a tramp], I might be killed any time.

I'd rather be in the army than outside where I was so raggedy and didn't have no jobs. I was glad to put on a United States Army uniform and get some food. I didn't care about the rifle what scared me. In the army, I wasn't gettin' killed on a train, I wasn't gonna starve. I felt proud to salute and look around and see all the good soldiers of the United States. I was a good soldier and got five battle stars. I'd rather be in the army now than see another Depression.

Looking Back—and Forward

Eyewitness accounts and memories of the Depression loom large in this book. They give some idea of the impact the Depression made on people's lives, in terms of poverty, unemployment, and leaving or losing a home. They show how some people protested and blamed governments, while others blamed themselves and felt ashamed of being unemployed. They suggest that almost everybody felt better when able to work, and even an evil regime such as **Nazi** Germany won wide support when it created jobs.

Such vivid sources must not let us forget the relatively undramatic lives lived by many people who stayed in their jobs. However, records show that the Depression had deep and long-lasting effects. Governments and peoples were determined not to let it happen again. In the 1940s, John Keynes's ideas were recognized (see page 30) and he became the driving force in setting up international agencies to keep the world economy in good order. Meanwhile, in many countries, the buying and selling of **shares** was more carefully controlled, and banks were insured by governments. Governments intervened more in economic affairs. **Social security** arrangements tended to become more thorough, and unemployment was kept down.

Even so, fears of another Depression lasted for a long time. They gradually faded as Europe and the United States prospered for decades, and beginning in the 1980s, many controls and regulations were given up. Overall, **prosperity** continued, but there were some severe ups and downs that—rightly or wrongly—revived old fears.

Sydney, Australia, is home to a modern **stock exchange**. High-tech equipment, such as computers and handheld devices, makes it possible to do even more business than in the past.

John Derden's poem

This is part of "What We Did For A Dollar A Day," a poem by John Derden, who was in the Civilian Conservation Corps (CCC) from 1937 to 1939. Though not a very sophisticated poem, it captures the atmosphere of the times.

In the depth of the Great Depression in 1933,
President Roosevelt created the CCC.
For our nation, he had a plan—
To give young men jobs, improve our forests, and build state and
    federal parks throughout the land.
From the country, villages, towns, large cities, and the ghettos, by the
    thousands we came.
We were eager to participate in FDR's CCC game.
Our uniforms and equipment were 1917 army style.
And every time we went to town, the girls would point to our
    pistol-legged trousers and smile.
We lived in tents and barracks and had to sweep the floors and make
    up our bed.
We shined our shoes, brushed our teeth, and combed our head.
To heat the barracks we built our own fires and cut our own wood.
The need for dry kindling was well understood.
They taught us to lay rock, pour cement, and build lakes for wild
    geese and ducks,
To operate bulldozers and drive trucks.
We dug ditches, built roads, and sloped banks,
Built campgrounds, log cabins, and water tanks.
We worked in the rain, the snow, and the mud,
To crush rock, cut logs, and rescue people from the Mississippi flood.
Our camps were located all across the land
From Alaska to Death Valley's burning sand.

Timeline

1914–1918 World War I: Britain, France, and the U.S. defeat Germany and its allies.

1917   **Communists** seize power in Russia, which is known from 1922 on as the Soviet Union, or **U.S.S.R.**

1921   A brief **recession** in the United States is followed by years of spectacular growth and **prosperity.**

1923   Defeated Germany suffers terrible **inflation.**

1926   A **general strike** takes place in Britain.

1929   Herbert Hoover becomes president of the United States.
The U.S. economy begins to slow down. The Wall Street Crash occurs in October. The United States withdraws loans from Europe.
The first Soviet Five-Year Plan begins.

1930   Prices of food and raw materials fall everywhere.
In industrialized countries, production falls and unemployment rises quickly. The United States introduces **tariffs** to protect its industries, starting a worldwide trend that causes world trade to shrink further.

1931   Panics and bank failures occur in Central Europe. Government spending is slashed in Great Britain, followed by a financial crisis.

1932   The Ottawa Conference is held and a tariff system is adopted by which Britain and the territories in its empire favor trading with one another (an arrangement known as Imperial Preference).
The Bonus Army is driven from Washington, D.C.
Unemployment and **Nazi** vote peak in Germany.

1933   Hitler takes power in Germany.
Franklin D. Roosevelt becomes president of the United States; the New Deal begins.

1935   For the third season in a row, dust storms blow across the Great Plains of the United States, intensifying the Dust Bowl crisis.
Italy invades Abyssinia (Ethiopia).

1936   The Jarrow March, the best known of British hunger marches, occurs.

1937   The Roosevelt Depression begins.

1938   Nazi Germany absorbs Austria and large areas of Czechoslovakia.

1939   Germany absorbs the rest of Czechoslovakia, and then invades Poland. Britain and France declare war on Germany: World War II begins.

1941   Japanese forces attack the American Pacific Fleet in Pearl Harbor, Oahu, Hawaii, causing the United States to enter the war.
Demand for military manpower and war production ends the Depression.

List of Primary Sources

The author and publisher gratefully acknowledge the following publications and websites from which written sources in the book are drawn. In some cases the wording or sentence structure has been simplified to make the material more appropriate for a school readership.

p. 9 Herbert Hoover, Inaugural Address, March 4, 1929.

p. 11 J. J. Raskob, interviewed by Samuel Crowther, "Everybody Ought to be Rich." (*Ladies' Home Journal*, August 1929).

p. 13 G. Bry, *Wages in Germany, 1871–1945* (Princeton University Press, 1960) acknowledged by my source, J. W. Hiden, *The Weimar Republic* (Longman, 1974, p. 86).

p. 15 *New York Times*, October 25, 1929.

p. 17 Edmund Wilson, *The American Earthquake* (W. H. Allen, 1958).

p. 19 Interview in *The People's Century*, PBS TV series, "Breadline" episode.

p. 21 Wal Hannington, *Never on Our Knees* (Lawrence and Wishart, 1967).

p. 23 Max Cohen, *I Was One of the Unemployed* (Gollancz, 1945).

p. 25 Paul Taylor, "Again the Covered Wagon," in *Survey Graphic* magazine, July 1935.

p. 27 Margery Spring Rice, *Working-Class Women* (Penguin, 1939; reissued by Virago, 1981).

p. 29 Christopher Isherwood, *Goodbye to Berlin* (Chatto and Windus, 1939).

p. 31 David Lloyd George's Election Address, 1929.

p. 33 G. Rees, BBC Archive disc, cited in Theo Barker (ed.), *The Long March of Everyman* (Andre Deutsch and the BBC, 1975).

p. 35 Ellen Wilkinson, *The Town that Was Murdered* (Gollancz, 1939).

p. 37 Robert L. Miller, "It's a Great Life": National Archives and Records Administration, Record Group 35, Division of Selection, "Success Stories." (Publisher CCC in Utah. Type: essay.)

p. 39 Albert Speer, *Inside the Third Reich.* (Weidenfeld, 1970).

p. 41 J. V. Stalin, *Works* volume 13 (Lawrence and Wishart, 1958).

p. 43 J. B. Priestley, *English Journey* (Heinemann, 1934).

p. 45 James Agee and Walker Evans, *Let Us Now Praise Famous Men* (Houghton Mifflin, 1941).

p. 47 and 49 Studs Terkel, *Hard Times: An Oral History of the Great Depression* Pantheon, 1970.

p. 51 John Derden, "*What We Did for a Dollar a Day*." Copyright John Justin 1998–2002. James F. Justin Civilian Conservation Corps Museum. [information from website members.aol.com/famjustin/derden1.html]

Sources for Further Research

Cohen, Robert, Ed. *Dear Mrs. Roosevelt: Letters from Children of the Great Depression.* Chapel Hill, N.C.: University of North Carolina Press, 2002.

Damon, Duane. *Headin' for Better Times: The Arts of the Great Depression.* Minneapolis, Minn.: Lerner Publishing Group, 2001.

Downing, David. *The Great Depression.* Chicago: Heinemann Library, 2001.

Nishi, Dennis. *Life During the Great Depression.* Farmington Hills, Mich.: Gale Group, 1997.

Ross, Stewart. *The Great Depression.* Chicago: Raintree Publishers, 1998.

Ruth, Amy. *Growing Up in the Great Depression, 1929–1941.* Minneapolis, Minn.: Lerner Publishing Group, 2002.

Stone, Tanya Lee. *The Great Depression and World War II.* Chicago: Raintree Publishers, 2001.

Wroble, Lisa A. *The New Deal and the Great Depression in American History.* Berkeley Heights, N.J.: Enslow Publishers, 2002.

Glossary

alliance agreement between countries to support one another

bankrupt officially unable to pay debts

boom strong or rapid economic growth or rise in share values

capital money or resources

capitalism economic system in which private firms and individuals own most resources and produce and trade for their own benefit

communism economic and political system in which the state, or society, owns most resources and controls the way they are produced and distributed

debacle complete defeat or collapse, leading to chaos

democracy government by the people or their elected representatives

dividend payment made to shareholders out of a company's profits

evicted officially forced to move out of a place you occupy

export good sold to another country

fascism political system based on dictatorship and military-style organization

fresco painting on a wall or ceiling

general strike simultaneous strike of workers in all or most industries

import item bought from another country

inflation rising prices

investor person who buys shares in a company

manuscript handwritten document

Nazi Party German political party led by Adolf Hitler, in power from 1933 to 1945. Nazi policies triggered World War II.

nonprofit company that is not in business to make a profit

patrón boss or employer

pawn to leave an item with a person who then lends you money. To recollect the item, one must repay the person.

prejudice opinion formed before examining the facts, and so not based on facts or reason

primary producer country that produces foodstuffs and raw materials, as opposed to goods that have been manufactured

prosperity enjoying great wealth, success, or good fortune

recession economic downturn

reparations compensation. Germany was forced to pay reparations for the damage done by its forces during World War I.

shantytown during the Depression, large group of shacks put up by homeless people and made of cardboard, corrugated iron, or similar materials

sharecropper tenant farmer who farms land for the owner and is paid a share of the profits

share certificate sold by a company that gives the buyer a share in the company's ownership

shareholder person who owns shares

slump drastic fall in prosperity, production, and jobs

social security system in which people who are sick, unemployed, or elderly receive payments from the government

speculator person who buys shares. The word is used, disapprovingly, of people who buy in the hope of making money quickly; their rushes and panics can have serious economic effects.

standard of living average level of prosperity—what people can afford to buy—in an area or country

statistic group of related facts that have been obtained by analyzing information

stock exchange building where stocks and shares are bought and sold

strike when employees stop working in order to protest something

tariff tax on foreign goods coming into a country. Tariffs are often intended to make such imports more expensive, and therefore less attractive, than similar home-produced goods.

testimony formal statement, often in a court of law

U.S.S.R. Union of Soviet Socialist Republics, also called the Soviet Union. Former federation of Communist republics that split in December 1991 into 15 independent countries, of which Russia is the largest.

Index

BPMS MEDIA CENTER